PIONEERS
OF SCIENCE
FICTION

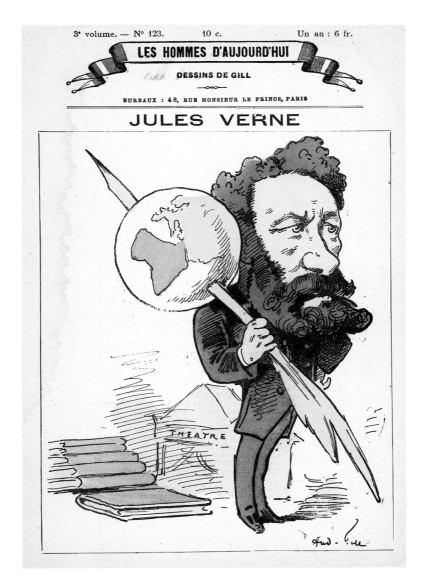

3e volume. — No 123.   10 c.   Un an : 6 fr.

LES HOMMES D'AUJOURD'HUI

DESSINS DE GILL

BUREAUX : 48, RUE MONSIEUR LE PRINCE, PARIS

JULES VERNE

THEATRE

BY JOHN HAMILTON

Vɪsɪᴛ ᴜs ᴀᴛ
WWW.ABDOPUBLISHING.COM

Published by ABDO Publishing Company, 4940 Viking Drive, Suite 622, Edina, Minnesota 55435.
Copyright ©2007 by Abdo Consulting Group, Inc. International copyrights reserved in all countries.
No part of this book may be reproduced in any form without written permission from the publisher.
ABDO & Daughters™ is a trademark and logo of ABDO Publishing Company.

Printed in the United States.

Editor: Paul Joseph
Graphic Design: John Hamilton
Cover Design: Neil Klinepier
Cover Illustration: Illustration from *The War of the Worlds*, Corbis
Interior Photos and Illustrations: p 1 caricature of Jules Verne, Mary Evans Picture Library; p 4
illustration from *Beowulf*, Mary Evans Picture Library; p 5 illustration from *The Tempest*, Mary Evans
Picture Library; p 6 Mary Shelley, Corbis; p 7 scene from *Bride of Frankenstein*, Getty Images; p 8 Edgar
Allan Poe, Corbis; p 9 illustration from *The Pit and the Pendulum*, Mary Evans Picture Library; p 10
illustration from *From the Earth to the Moon*, Corbis; p 11 Jules Verne, Getty Images; p 12 Jules Verne,
Getty Images; p 13 collection of Verne's books, Getty Images; p 14 illustration from *Twenty Thousand
Leagues Under the Sea*, Corbis; p 15 illustration from *Twenty Thousand Leagues Under the Sea*, Corbis;
p 16 scene from *Mysterious Island*, courtesy Crown Media; p 17 illustration from *Twenty Thousand Leagues
Under the Sea*, Getty Images; p 18 illustration from *The War of the Worlds*, Corbis; p 19 H. G. Wells,
Getty Images; p 20 (top) young H. G. Wells, Mary Evans Picture Library; p 20 (bottom) London Bridge,
Corbis; p 21 scene from *Things to Come*, Getty Images; p 22 H. G. Wells in library, Getty Images; p 23
scene from *The Invisible Man*, Corbis; p 24 lobby poster for *The War of the Worlds*, Getty Images; p 25
illustration from *The War of the Worlds*, Corbis; p 26 Arthur Conan Doyle, Getty Images; p 27 illustration
from *The Lost World*, Mary Evans Picture Library; p 28 Edgar Rice Burroughs, Getty Images; p 29 cover
of 1927 issue of *Amazing Stories*, Mary Evans Picture Library.

Library of Congress Cataloging-in-Publication Data

Hamilton, John, 1959-
  Pioneers of science fiction / John Hamilton.
    p. cm. -- (The world of science fiction)
  Includes index.
  ISBN-13: 978-1-59679-992-9
  ISBN-10: 1-59679-992-7
 1. Science fiction, English--History and criticism--Juvenile literature. 2. Science fiction, American--
History and criticism--Juvenile literature. 3. Authors, English--Biography--Juvenile literature. 4. Authors,
American--Biography--Juvenile literature. I. Title. II. Series.

PR106.H36 2007
823'.0876209--dc22
  [B]
                        2006012003

CONTENTS

THE PIONEERS

Science fiction, as the great writer and teacher James Gunn once said, is the fiction of ideas. Other kinds of fiction get their strength from plots and characters. Of course, plots and characters are important in science fiction. But science fiction is a forward-looking genre, or category, of literature. We're interested in these stories because we want to see how science and technology will affect us in the future. Will we ever discover aliens? Will robots outgrow their masters and rule the earth? Will people someday land on other planets, such as Mars? In science fiction, the idea is king.

Writers have been thinking about these kinds of ideas for many years. A few scholars think the earliest science fiction was written centuries ago. They say that stories such as William Shakespeare's *The Tempest*, or even the ancient Norse saga *Beowulf*, have fantastic elements that qualify them as science fiction. In *The Tempest*, a sorcerer named Prospero and his daughter are shipwrecked on an island in the Adriatic Sea. The play has magic, sprites and fairies, witches, and a deformed creature called Caliban. The epic poem *Beowulf*, which may be more than 1,000 years old, is about a group of Norse adventurers who travel to Denmark and do battle with a hideous monster that's terrorizing the countryside.

Both *Beowulf* and *The Tempest* are out-of-this-world stories that rely strongly on fantasy. Tales like this are sometimes called *proto*-science fiction. Proto means "the first," or "primitive." But science fiction is more than just fantasy. That's why most people who study literature reject these early tales as science fiction. Science fiction needs *science* to make its magic. It needs an *idea*, a speculation of how science and technology affect our society. That's the reason why science fiction is often called *speculative fiction*. True science fiction would come later, when science and human culture began to collide, with earth-shaking results.

Facing page: Ariel, a winged sprite, pinches the ear of the creature Caliban in this scene from William Shakespeare's *The Tempest*, with art by Arthur Rackham. *Below:* The Danish warrior Beowulf battles a dragon in this scene from *Beowulf*.

5

MARY SHELLEY

By the early 19ᵗʰ century, the Industrial Revolution was in full swing. After thousands of years of farming and manual labor, society began to change. Scientific advances—steam power, for example—made industry and manufacturing much more important. Many people lost their jobs, or were trapped in nightmarish factories that treated workers more like animals than human beings.

People began realizing how important science was to their lives. Many worried about how they would be affected. It seemed that science was moving at breathtaking speed. The future might be wondrous, but many feared instead that it would lead to disaster.

Below: Mary Shelley, author of *Frankenstein*.

In 1816, English novelist Mary Wollstonecraft Shelley wrote a book called *Frankenstein, or, The Modern Prometheus*. It was a tale of terror that many scholars and authors say was the first true science fiction novel.

Shelley wrote *Frankenstein* when she was only 19 years old. She and her future husband, the famous English poet Percy Shelley, were staying at a villa near Geneva, Switzerland, with another poet, Lord George Byron, and his personal physician, William Polidori. A long stretch of cold and dreary weather had forced the group indoors, where they entertained themselves by reading ghost stories. One night they decided to have a contest to see who could write the scariest story.

Mary Shelley got her inspiration from a nightmare, in which she saw a troubled man kneeling beside a creature, a horror created by his own two hands. With this seed of an idea, Shelley feverishly wrote her novel. The story is about a deranged scientist, Victor Frankenstein, who uses modern technology to create life. Wielding this God-like power, he animates the shell of a creature cobbled together from dead body parts:

Above: A scene from 1935's *Bride of Frankenstein*, starring Boris Karloff as the creature.

"It was on a dreary night of November, that I beheld the accomplishment of my toils. … It was already one in the morning; the rain pattered dismally against the panes, and my candle was nearly burnt out, when, by the glimmer of the half-extinguished light, I saw the dull yellow eye of the creature open; it breathed hard, and a convulsive motion agitated its limbs."

The scientist recoils in horror at his creation. Panic-stricken, Frankenstein runs away. The creature, abandoned and unloved by everyone it meets, finally seeks revenge against its creator.

Mary Shelley's writing was influenced by many sources, especially the Gothic, gloomy literature of her time. It's also possible that she suffered from depression after giving birth to a stillborn baby the year before. Whatever the cause, the nightmare vision that stirred her to write *Frankenstein* became one of the most popular stories of its time. More than two centuries later, writers and filmmakers continue to produce countless remakes and sequels.

People identify with *Frankenstein's* main theme. It is a warning to mankind not to "overreach," not to blindly use new technology without understanding the consequences. Like any good science fiction story, *Frankenstein* is about an idea: science can do great harm when used in the blind pursuit of power.

EDGAR ALLAN POE

Above: Edgar Allan Poe, one of the founding fathers of science fiction. *Facing page:* An Arthur Rackham illustration from a 1935 edition of Poe's *The Pit and the Pendulum*, showing walls of burning iron driving a prisoner towards the center of his cell and the deadly brink of the bottomless pit.

Edgar Allan Poe was born January 19, 1809, in Boston, Massachusetts. By the time he was two, his father had abandoned the family, and his mother had died of tuberculosis. Young Poe went to live with John and Frances Allan, of Richmond, Virginia. Poe's middle name is taken from his foster parents.

At different points in his life, Poe lived in London, Baltimore, and New York City. He also served in the United States Army, attending the U.S. Military Academy at West Point.

As a young man in Baltimore, Poe wrote fiction to support himself. His stories became very popular. Much of his work had a "macabre" style that explored themes of death and dread. Short stories and poems such as *The Raven*, *The Fall of the House of Usher*, and *The Pit and the Pendulum* cemented his reputation as a great figure of American literature.

In addition to his tales of horror and suspense, Poe is also one of the "founding fathers" of science fiction. Stories such as *Hans Pfaall* (space flight) and *A Tale of Ragged Mountains* (time travel) were scientifically serious, based on a rational understanding of our world. In *Hans Pfaall*, the hero takes a journey to the moon.

Poe wasn't the first writer to describe a trip into space. But other writers of the time used fanciful methods, such as hitching a ride on a high-flying goose. Poe, on the other hand, avoided the supernatural. He instead used the best understanding of astronomy at that time. His science fiction stories, though fantastic, had the appearance of being true. In literature this is called "verisimilitude."

Verisimilitude is a very important part of most science fiction, separating it from pure fantasy. Poe influenced many science fiction writers who would come later, including Jules Verne and H. G. Wells. Edgar Allan Poe died October 7, 1849. The exact cause of his death is unknown, a final puzzle to this fascinating man of mystery.

JULES VERNE

Jules Verne was one of science fiction's most important authors. He firmly established science fiction as a category (a genre) of literature, even more so than Edgar Allan Poe. And even though Verne admitted he was heavily influenced by Poe, most people today think of Verne as the "father" of science fiction. In his stories, he predicted the invention of many modern devices, including missiles, airplanes, and televisions. His tales of adventure took readers all over the earth, even far below and above it. He was wildly popular, and remains so today. His many books have been translated into more than 112 languages.

Jules Gabriel Verne was born on February 8, 1828, in the harbor city of Nantes, France. He was the oldest of five children.

As a boy, Verne's imagination ran wild as he watched ships navigating the Loire River close to his home. One story that is often told about Verne claims that when he was 11, he wanted to be a sailor, so he stowed away on a ship bound for Asia. His furious father, however, was waiting for him when the ship reached the next port. Verne was punished, but he never lost his thirst for adventure. He promised from then on that he would travel only in his imagination. Verne kept his promise, writing more than 80 books in his lifetime.

Left: An illustration from Verne's 1865 novel, *From the Earth to the Moon.*
Facing page: Jules Verne, the father of science fiction.

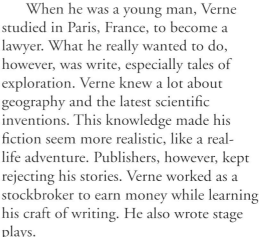

When he was a young man, Verne studied in Paris, France, to become a lawyer. What he really wanted to do, however, was write, especially tales of exploration. Verne knew a lot about geography and the latest scientific inventions. This knowledge made his fiction seem more realistic, like a real-life adventure. Publishers, however, kept rejecting his stories. Verne worked as a stockbroker to earn money while learning his craft of writing. He also wrote stage plays.

In 1863, Verne met Pierre-Jules Hetzel, an important French publisher. Hetzel liked Verne's stories, but thought they needed some changes. Verne was happy to take Hetzel's advice. He put a little comedy

Above: Jules Verne's first big success came after *Five Weeks in a Balloon* was published in 1863.

into his plots, changed his endings to make them happier, and left out a lot of the politics that offended previous editors.

That year, Hetzel published Verne's *Five Weeks in a Balloon*. It was an adventure novel about a scientist and two companions who explore Africa in a hydrogen-filled balloon. It was an instant hit with the reading public. Pierre-Jules Hetzel was so delighted that he offered the young writer a hefty salary for 20 years, in exchange for producing two novels a year, to first be published in monthly installments in a magazine produced by Hetzel (*Magazine d'Education et de Récréation*), followed later in book form. It was a very successful arrangement for both men.

After *Five Weeks in a Balloon*, Verne was free to write the kinds of stories that interested him the most, which included Verne's predictions of new scientific inventions. Many people in the late 19th century were optimistic that science and technology would lift mankind to new heights and a brighter future. Verne touched a nerve with readers.

In Verne's time, the term "science fiction" hadn't been invented yet. Pierre-Jules Hetzel called Verne's stories, "novels of a new type," and advertised them as *voyages extraordinaires* (extraordinary voyages). The public couldn't get enough of his writing, which made Verne rich and wildly popular.

In 1864, Verne published *A Journey to the Center of the Earth*. In this science fiction novel, Professor Otto Lidenbrock leads an expedition down a shaft formed by a volcano in Iceland. The group travels to the center of the earth, encountering bottomless caverns and dangerous geysers. Rafting upon an ocean within the earth, they dodge prehistoric beasts and giant insects. Finally, they are sent violently upwards in a magma-filled rock chimney. After a terrifying ride, they are ejected back on the surface, through a hole in the side of a volcano—in Italy! They have indeed traveled through the center of the earth, emerging on the other side of the world, frazzled but safe.

For his next novel, Verne took his fictional adventurers in the opposite direction, into outer space. In 1865, he published *From the Earth to the Moon*. The novel is about a group of adventurers who build an enormous cannon that can fire a spaceship to the moon. Verne predicted many things about space travel that would be proven correct nearly 100 years after the book was written. He described the weightlessness of space. Also, his fictional spaceship blasted off from Florida, just like NASA spaceships do today.

Above: A collection of Verne's books, advertised with the slogan, *Voyages Extraordinaires*.

Many readers think *Twenty Thousand Leagues Under the Sea* is Jules Verne's greatest work of science fiction. The 1870 novel tells the underwater adventure of marine biologist Professor Aronnax, together with his trusty servant Conseil, and whaling harpooner Ned Land. On an expedition to investigate the mysterious sinking of several ocean-going ships, the trio are themselves shipwrecked. They are soon taken aboard an advanced, futuristic submarine called *Nautilus.* The ship's creator is the mysterious, fanatical Captain Nemo. (Nemo means "no one" in Latin.) Nemo reveals to them that *Nautilus* is electrically powered. The secretive captain and his crew roam the ocean depths, conducting marine biology research.

Captain Nemo is a brooding, complex character. He has a thirst for scientific knowledge. He is a renegade, a genius inventor, musician, and book collector. But he also hates civilization. He sinks surface ships by ramming them with the steel-reinforced bow of the *Nautilus.* The novel never reveals Nemo's past, or the dark secret that fills him with such hatred and madness. But there is no doubt that he is in full command of his underwater world. "I am the law, I am justice," he declares to Professor Aronnax.

Nemo tells his guests they can never leave *Nautilus.* He fears that if they return to civilization, they will reveal the strange captain's existence. The rest of the book is filled with underwater adventure: hunting for food at the bottom of the ocean; visiting the submerged lost city of Atlantis; sailing under the Antarctic ice shelves; and even a burial within a coral wilderness. At one point, the crew of the *Nautilus* battles a giant squid, a *devilfish:*

"By then the Nautilus had returned to the surface of the waves. Stationed on the top steps, one of the seamen undid the bolts of the hatch. But he had scarcely unscrewed the nuts when the hatch flew up with tremendous violence, obviously pulled open by the suckers on a devilfish's arm.

"Instantly one of those long arms glided like a snake into the opening, and twenty others were quivering above. With a sweep of the ax, Captain Nemo chopped off this fearsome tentacle, which slid writhing down the steps.

"Just as we were crowding each other to reach the platform, two more arms lashed the air, swooped on the seaman stationed in front of Captain Nemo, and carried the fellow away with irresistible violence.

"Captain Nemo gave a shout and leaped outside. We rushed after him."

Above: A scene from the 2005 Hallmark Channel television adaptation of Jules Verne's *Mysterious Island.*
Facing page: Captain Nemo and his crew battle a giant squid in this illustration by Zdenek Burian from *Twenty Thousand Leagues Under the Sea.*

After battling the squid, the trio of adventurers eventually manage to make it home safely, but the fate of Captain Nemo and the *Nautilus* are not revealed (until Verne's sequel, *The Mysterious Island*, in 1875).

At the time Verne wrote *Twenty Thousand Leagues Under the Sea*, submarines were a brand new technology. Nothing yet existed like Verne's *Nautilus*, a machine-powered, ocean-going submersible that could stay underwater for long periods of time, roam the seas, and attack enemy surface ships. In addition to firing the imagination of millions of readers, Verne's popular book inspired submarine inventors to experiment with more advanced designs.

As time went by, Verne continued writing his novels of *voyages extraordinaires*. After 20 years, when Verne's contract expired, his publisher, Pierre-Jules Hetzel, eagerly renewed it. Even after Hetzel's death, the publisher's son continued the arrangement with Verne.

Jules Verne wrote for more than 40 years, until his death on March 24, 1905. The science fiction pioneer's books are still popular today, more than 100 years after his death.

H.G. WELLS

H. G. Wells was one of the greatest science fiction writers of all time. His forward-thinking tales—he called them "scientific romances"—opened new worlds to the reading public. Science fiction author and teacher James Gunn called Wells, "the man who invented tomorrow."

Some of Wells' most important novels—*The Time Machine, The Island of Dr. Moreau, The Invisible Man, The First Men in the Moon, The War of the Worlds*—explore ideas that were called genius and visionary when they were first written. So many authors have followed Wells in the past half century, imitating and building upon his themes, that his ideas are now commonplace. Where would science fiction be today without Wells and his unique visions of the future?

Herbert George Wells was born on September 21, 1866, in Bromley, Kent, southeast of London. He was the youngest of four children, born to Sarah and Joseph Wells. They nicknamed their youngest son "Bertie."

Wells grew up in near-poverty. His father was a failed shopkeeper, his mother a maid. When he was seven years old, Wells broke his leg. It was a bad injury, and it took many weeks for him to recover. To pass the time, young Bertie read books—lots of them. He soon fell in love with the world's great works of fiction, and dreamed of someday being a writer himself. Wells later wrote that his broken leg was "one of the luckiest events of my life."

Left: An illustration from *The War of the Worlds,* showing a man encountering an invading Martian.
Facing page: Science fiction legend H. G. Wells.

When he was a teenager, his parents sent Wells to work as a draper's apprentice. It was a job he was ill suited for. He escaped a life of lower-middle class drudgery by becoming a teacher and studying science. Within a few years, Wells fulfilled his lifelong dream by becoming a journalist and a writer.

Wells was a skillful author, a master of his craft. In his novels, especially his early works, he wove deep symbolism into exciting stories. Wells wrote about two broad themes: hope for a better future, coupled with a fear that someday mankind would destroy itself.

Wells was often called the "English Jules Verne." But unlike Verne's stories, Wells populated his novels with seemingly ordinary people thrust into frightful situations. Jules Verne wrote adventure stories filled with technological marvels. By contrast, Wells focused on how the future would affect mankind. He foresaw how the world of the 20th century would change society. He worried about overcrowding and pollution, and he felt uneasy about the rapid rise of technology and scientific knowledge.

Wells was a didactic author, which means he liked to teach through his writing. His stories dazzled readers' imaginations, but they also contained a warning: there will be hidden consequences to the great scientific achievements of our age.

Above: Herbert George Wells, at the age of nine.
Below: London Bridge is clogged with pedestrians and traffic in this photograph from 1880.

Above: A scene from *Things to Come*, the 1936 movie version of H. G. Wells' 1933 novel, *The Shape of Things to Come.*

The Time Machine, published in 1895, was Wells' first novel. It's the book that made him famous, and remains popular even today. The story's narrator, identified only as the "time traveler," creates a time machine made of exotic metals and crystalline bars. Eager to see what the future holds, the time traveler increases the speed of his machine so that days pass in the blink of an eye. Soon, he finds himself in a world thousands of years in the future.

The time traveler learns that mankind has evolved into two separate species, the Eloi and the Morlocks. The Eloi are beautiful and childlike, while the Morlocks are deformed beasts who live beneath the earth. Descending into the Morlocks' underground lair to retrieve his stolen time machine, the time traveler learns that the light-sensitive Morlocks are cannibals who feed on the Eloi above.

Below: H. G. Wells in 1940. Late in his career he wrote about social change and world peace.

Wells grew up as a lower-class English citizen, looked down upon by people who had more money or status. Through his writing, Wells wanted to teach people the evil of this kind of class system. *The Time Machine* was a wild adventure story that people loved, but it also spoke harsh truths of how class systems can lead to horror and misery.

The following year, in 1896, Wells published *The Island of Dr. Moreau*. The novel tells the story of a man shipwrecked on an island, its animal-like inhabitants the result of cruel experiments conducted by the mysterious Dr. Moreau. Wells used the book to explore themes of society and human nature. It was also a stern warning about the dangers of reckless scientific research.

Wells' short novel, *The Invisible Man*, was published in 1897. The book's main character is a scientist who devises a way to make the human body completely transparent. He conducts an experiment on himself and becomes invisible. An unfortunate side effect, however, is that anyone becoming invisible also flirts with insanity.

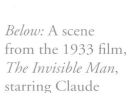

Below: A scene from the 1933 film, *The Invisible Man*, starring Claude Rains.

The War of the Worlds is an alien invasion novel first published in 1898. Many consider it Wells' best work. It is a terrifying book about Martians landing on Earth and attacking people with their superior technology. The great cities of the world, including London, fall under the scorching destruction of the Martian "heat rays." The human race is on the verge of extinction when, in one of the great plot twists of science fiction, the Martians begin dying out. The invaders have been infected by Earth germs, of which they have no natural defense. Humanity is saved by the smallest, humblest of creatures.

Later in his career, Wells concentrated less on science fiction and more on issues of social change and world peace. He was very influential, but today he is remembered mainly for his brilliant tales of science fiction. H. G. Wells died on August 13, 1946. His sympathy for ordinary people, and his optimism about the future of mankind, despite the dangers, make his stories entertaining and important even today.

Facing page: An illustration from a 1906 edition of Wells' novel, *The War of the Worlds,* showing Martian fighting machines attacking humans. *Below:* A lobby poster for the 1953 movie version of Wells' classic alien invasion story.

H·G·WELLS'

THE *War of the Worlds*

COLOR BY TECHNICOLOR

PRODUCED BY GEORGE PAL · DIRECTED BY BYRON HASKIN · SCREEN PLAY BY BARRE LYNDON · A PARAMOUNT PICTURE

ARTHUR CONAN DOYLE

Sir Arthur Conan Doyle was a Scottish writer born on May 22, 1859. He lived most of his life in Great Britain, until his death on July 7, 1930. Doyle is most famous for his stories about master detective Sherlock Holmes, but he also wrote many other kinds of novels, including science fiction.

Of all his creations, Doyle's favorite character was not Sherlock Holmes. Instead, he was more fond of Professor George Challenger, a sincere man of science, big as a bull, yet good-humored. The character first appeared in *The Lost World*, published in 1912. In the book, Professor Challenger organizes an expedition to a remote South American plateau where, he believes, live prehistoric creatures such as dinosaurs. Joining the professor on this dangerous journey are Professor Summerlee, adventurer Lord John Roxton, and journalist Ed Malone.

Below: Sir Arthur Conan Doyle, author of *The Lost World*.

After a long voyage, Challenger and his companions climb up the plateau. They discover a hidden world full of wonders and strange beasts. They are nearly eaten by dinosaurs, and also discover a race of hostile ape-men. After a series of harrowing adventures, the explorers barely escape the plateau with their lives. They return home to London with a small pterodactyl as proof of their adventure, but the winged dinosaur escapes. It is last observed flying across the light of the moon, never to be seen again.

Doyle continued the character of Professor Challenger with 1913's *The Poison Belt*, in which Earth's atmosphere is contaminated by a huge cloud of poisonous gas from outer space.

Challenger and his companions seal themselves in an airtight room in his house until the cloud passes, then emerge to find themselves the sole survivors. (Like H. G. Wells' *The War of the Worlds*, however, *The Poison Belt* contains a surprise ending.) Doyle's message was simple and direct: people need to appreciate the short time we have on this Earth, for the end may come at any time, with no warning.

In later years, Arthur Conan Doyle would write three more Professor Challenger novels. Sherlock Holmes will always be Doyle's biggest legacy, but he will also be remembered for his fantastic science fiction adventures.

Left: A pterodactyl seizes dinner from a group of explorers in this 1912 illustration of Arthur Conan Doyle's *The Lost World.*

EDGAR RICE BURROUGHS

Edgar Rice Burroughs was an American writer best known as the creator of *Tarzan of the Apes*. He was also famous for his wildly popular "Barsoom" series of science fiction books, which take place on the planet Mars.

Burroughs was born September 1, 1875, in Chicago, Illinois. By the time he was 35, he considered himself a failure. He'd been fruitless at many jobs, including work as a salesman, a gold miner, and a cowboy. By 1911, he was working as a pencil sharpener when he decided to try writing fiction. He declared, "… if people were paid for writing rot such as I read in some of those

Below: Edgar Rice Burroughs at work in his office.

magazines that I could write stories just as rotten. As a matter of fact, although I had never written a story, I knew absolutely that I could write stories just as entertaining... ." Burroughs' first novel, *Under the Moons of Mars*, was published in 1912 for the sum of $400. (The book was later re-titled *A Princess of Mars*.)

Under the Moons of Mars told the story of Captain John Carter, who is mysteriously transported to Barsoom. (Barsoom was Burroughs' name for the Red Planet). Carter is thrust into a series of fantastic adventures. He battles Tars Tarkas, a hostile green Martian who stands 15 feet (4.6 m) tall, has four arms, white tusks, and eyes on the end of long antennae. Carter eventually becomes Warlord of Mars, and marries the beautiful princess Deja Thoris.

That same year, Burroughs became famous for Tarzan, making him one of the most popular authors in the country. Tarzan was his main claim to fame, but Burroughs' science fiction stories were so well-liked that he continued to revisit Mars in 10 more books. He also wrote a series of books that take place on Venus, as well as two books set on Earth's moon. In 1924, Burroughs wrote the science fiction classic, *The Land That Time Forgot*, about a submarine crew that stumbles upon a hidden island in which dinosaurs and other primitive creatures roam free.

Edgar Rice Burroughs was an extraordinary storyteller. He wrote more than 90 books, entertaining millions of readers. Many of his science fiction stories have been turned into Hollywood movies. Burroughs died on March 19, 1950, at the age of 74.

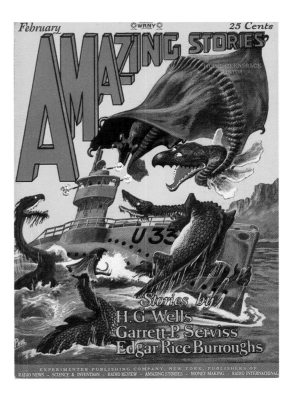

Right: The cover of the February 1927 issue of *Amazing Stories* featured a scene from Burroughs' *The Land That Time Forgot*, by artist Frank R. Paul.

GLOSSARY

ASTRONOMY

The scientific study of the universe, including the stars and planets, how they were formed, how they move, and their composition and size.

DIDACTIC

Intending to teach, especially giving moral instruction. For example, H. G. Wells is often called a didactic writer. His stories are thrilling adventures, but Wells also intended to teach his readers about the hidden dangers of the rapid rise of technology.

GENRE

A type, or kind, or a work of art. In literature, a genre is distinguished by a common subject, theme, or style. Some genres include science fiction, fantasy, and mystery.

GOTHIC

A type of literature, which was especially popular in the late 18th and 19th centuries, that uses remote settings and sinister atmosphere to suggest horror and mystery. Mary Wollstonecraft Shelley was heavily influenced by the Gothic style of literature when she wrote *Frankenstein* in 1816.

INDUSTRIAL REVOLUTION

The rapid development of industry that happened in the late 18th and early 19th centuries, especially in Great Britain and other Western countries. The Industrial Revolution is usually characterized by steam power, the growth of factories, and mass-manufactured goods. Science fiction became popular as science and manufacturing became more and more important in people's lives.

MACABRE

Something gruesome and horrible. Macabre literature is horrifying because of its depiction of death or injury. Edgar Allan Poe often wrote macabre stories.

NASA
The National Aeronautics and Space Administration. NASA is the United States' main space agency, responsible for programs such as the Space Shuttle and unmanned space probes.

NORSE
The people, language, or culture of Scandinavia, especially medieval Scandinavia. The Vikings were famous Nordic people.

PROMETHEUS
Prometheus was a Greek demigod, one of the Titans, who stole fire from Zeus in heaven and brought it back to Earth to benefit mankind. As punishment, Zeus had Prometheus chained to a rock, where a vulture came each day to eat his liver, which grew back every night. He was eventually rescued by Hercules. When Mary Shelley named her novel, *Frankenstein, or, the Modern Prometheus*, she meant that Dr. Frankenstein, like all of mankind, can do great harm in the blind pursuit of power.

SAGA
A long, involved story where a hero achieves something important. They are often seen in medieval Norse stories, such as old Viking sagas.

SPECULATION
To guess, or form a theory, about what will happen, without firm evidence. Science fiction is often called speculative fiction, because its authors are making guesses about the future, usually based on trends they see happening today.

VERISIMILITUDE
Something that has the appearance of being true, or real.

INDEX